Poems my cauldron

Lucy Gabriel.

Published by Lucy Gabriel
Lucygabriel.cauldron@outlook.com

Cover photograph and design by Michael Burgess
michaelburgess@live.co.uk

All rights reserved.
Copyright©2023

The right of Lucy Gabriel to be identified as the author of this work has been asserted in accordance with the Copyright, Designs and Patent Act 1988.

No part of this book may be reproduced in whole or part in any form or by any means, electronic or mechanical, or by any information storage and retrieval system without the written permission of the author.

Poems from my cauldron

Lucy Gabriel

Writings from the depths of my heart, soul and being

CONTENTS

1) My dad had a heart and soul
2) I still miss the purity
3) These broken pieces
4) I dream of you
5) Last night I dreamed of you
6) My Valentine's day card
7) Today I return to the sea
8) Sea poem September
9) The last day by the sea
10) I need to go to the woods
11) We know so little of our earth lineages
12) To feel what I know
13) I need grounding
14) I only got here yesterday
15) Sing-back life into the sacred sites.
16) Every sacred forest
17) The trees are sleeping
18) I dive deep
19) A black rock
20) I sit on the back of an eagle
21) I love Cornwall
22) Waiting for the rain
23) There's a massive shifting going on
24) I'm in love with the world
25) The bond a woman may have with a cat
26) I'm a lone witch walking
27) I have always loved to write
28) There's a very fine line
29) I'm the kind of woman
30) On the day of a funeral
31) In a past-life regression
32) Disconnecting from the cogs and gears
33) I do not bathe every day

34) I spend so little time alone
35) The wheel turns to the autumn equinox
36) Samhain
37) I'm finding my tribe now
38) The total silence of a quiet house.
39) I am a lone witch walking
40) The company of women
41) I trust a circle of women
42) The media tells older women
43) On women's day
44) I am a rebellious woman
45) I am growing
46) I reached down into my innermost Self
47) Approaching the year's ynd
48) Christmas Day
49) Over the Last Year
50) My writing event is booked
51) I've reached the end of the winter
52) There's nothing to fear
53) My ancestors and past lives
54) I want to step out of the Circus
55) It's my Birthday
56) Save your tears, don't cry now
57) As in Rome so in the modern Empire today.
58) Who to trust ?
59) We are living in a techno nightmare
60) Society functions by silencing
61) Free running gossamer threads
62) It fails and falters
63) I'm settled
64) I've become real
65) Where can I find you
66) My ideal sacred male.
67) I manifest you
68) I'm a freelance, a maverick

69) I'm here in your bed
70) I'm so glad I have you

Acknowledgments

I would like to thank the following people for their support and help, and for believing in me enough to help this book become a reality, a dream I thought could never come true. To Fiona and Danny for always being solidly by my side, encouraging me. For Wendy, Gwen and Rose-Marie, my sisters. For my parents, children and grandchildren, and all the ancestors that went before us. For Sue, whose creative writing group sustained me. For Win, who helped me untangle a bunch of writings into a cohesive order. And great and heartfelt thanks to Michael for all his expertise and experience in the world of books, and for the patient time spent editing with me and on my behalf through all 5 drafts.

Introduction

Welcome to my collection of poems.

The death of my father and betrayal by one I loved deeply cast me into a place of darkness and loss like I had never felt before.

My long dark night of the soul became my hero's journey, bringing me new life and deeper understanding.

I have catalogued my process in these poems over a year or more and discovered kindred spirits, renewed purpose and a deeper connection with the worlds of nature and spirit.

I am deeply thankful to be blessed with the ability to articulate my experiences in order to share them with a wider selection of lovely people.

I dedicate this book to everyone who understands anything described herein

Blessings upon you all.

Lucy

1
My dad had a heart and soul.

My dad had a heart and soul.
He kept both well guarded
Lest they expose any weakness.
Any chink in his armour
Which could be exploited.
No showing his softness
Or triggering a meltdown.
Sometimes I remember him
Getting so angry and frustrated with me
That he would, in extremis, cry.

This always made me feel extra guilty.
He shared my interest in the esoteric,
The mistrust of the Tories;
I know he could have spoken of
The deepest stirrings of his heart,
The things he felt so strongly
But he felt safer?
In control?
More of a man ?
That these things remained under lock and key.

Except on occasions they overflowed.
I saw him watch a documentary,
About young WW1 soldiers
Being sent
Over the top
To their inevitable and pointless deaths.
He had tears running down his face.
Sobbing from his soul for the evil being done.

My dad was a fully paid up
Member of the human race;
Yet, fearful of the repercussions
Of his passions being expressed
He instead repressed.
Held them in.
I had an angry shadow for a father.
A physical presence which
Rarely allowed me to connect with it
Though I made huge efforts to do so.

This played out in my life.

I had found men, I thought,

like my Father.
But they lacked his hidden passions and depths.
The best and rarest feature about him
And were merely emotionally dead.
They didn't understand
That what I sought so desperately…
Needed most
Was just to touch souls.

Dad, A year since you admitted
That I have always been exactly like you,
Before you left forever -
I have begun to understand.
I mourn for your loss,
But the far greater loss
Is the friendship and connection
We could have had.
And I really, really tried.

2

I still miss the purity of what I had with you.

I still miss the purity of what I had with you.

I feel like part of me has darkened

And gone into hiding and sadness,

Without your playful spirit to enjoy.

The wound is bigger than you yourself could make

For it represents that which I ever sought

To feel complete;

To light up all my circuits as nobody else ever did.

I thought I found my other half, separated by Zeus.

I tended to your wounds,

You understood little of this world either

But I healed and taught you all I know;

And I loved you like a child.

Ferociously I cared for and encouraged you,

Blended my body with yours

In a way that was electrifying

Nothing else mattered.

I can still feel the wound

It is smaller but will never heal completely.

The bond we had was deeper than this life
We knew each other deeply,
Yet now I work alone
While you do, I know not what, or where.
You brightened my life;
Entertained and saw a side of me
I can so rarely express.
You listened, adored and loved me
And were my enchanting muse.
Now you are gone,
Dancing away after the bright lights
Of the travelling carnival
While my house is in darkness.
Sometimes you still sing in my head
When you need or miss me,
But I have to ignore your call.
I cannot bear your nearness without your intimacy
The pain of all that went before
Still pulls my heart.
I can have no more to do with you.
For this lifetime at least
It's over.

3

The broken pieces inside still hurt.

The broken pieces inside still hurt.
In the stillness, the pieces rattled together
Like a broken Christmas bauble;
Delicate pieces of a beautiful whole
Now sharp shards to be handled with care;
Cutting not only her fingers,
But those of any who tried to get close enough
To feel the place of pain.
She didn't know what to do.
It had been a long time now
Since she felt whole.
That joie de vivre once shared with another
Was now sealed in another glass bauble
That she could no longer reach into,
Preserved only for posterity;
Another time that she could no longer touch
And only fleetingly remember.
The sea brought solace,
As she always did
On a deep and fulfilling level;
Yet she felt fully the illusion of her separateness

So keenly it cut her to the bones
Like the bitter winter wind,
That tugged at her scarf and coat tails.
Love was a trick, she knew that much.
A wonderful spell
That lifted you up on high
And gave a transcendent feeling
That reminded her of home…
The soul family in another dimension
Who never let her down
And the reason she came here
To feel impermanence, change, separation
To stand on ones own feet
Unsure of who to trust.
Few were worthy she had found,
Many did not understand her ways.
Her words, though articulate
Dropped mute like stones
In front of the uncomprehending people here.
This was their world not hers, after all.
She was weird, a misfit
In a world of earthly woes
Missing the place where all the pieces fitted.

The task, if any, was forgotten for now
As she watched the waves glint in the darkness,
By the light of the treacherous moon
Who distorted the perceptions,
And cast a glamour on things mundane
So that they became desirable.
She sighed, dropped the letter folded into a boat
Into the troubled waves,
And turned quickly towards home;
Her tears as salty as the ocean, adrift on the tide
Of her own turbulent emotions,
With only her innermost soul to guide her.
She must learn to listen,
To have faith;
To give up trying to write her own narrative
And learn to be subject to destiny.
Always being in the place she needs to be,
And to know she would not only heal,
But emerge as more complete than she was before.
Relationships are to teach,
Not to make us any more than fleetingly happy,
Here on this blighted star.

4

A dream of you, my faithless lover.

A dream of you, my faithless lover.
We are in a pub,
And my drink contains broken glass.
You attempt once again to justify yourself,
I ask you to keep your voice down and whisper.
I have a baby to take care of,
Which isn't mine but is my responsibility.
You are still disloyal
The bond between us broken long ago.
Strong as spiders silk yet delicate and fragile
In need of loving attention.

You begin to justify yourself again,
And I notice your mistress
Sitting behind you at the next table
Getting ready to leave.
She rises and tells you she is going
To catch the bus to someplace else,
And obedient as a dog
You go to her immediately
To wait at the bus stop together.

Even though she doesn't want you
While I gather up my baby
And go look for my car.

You hardly even notice I am going
So wrapped up in her attention are you,
And I have to shout your name
And say "I'm going now".
You nod and turn straight back to her
And once again I am made nothing
Despite the amazing love we once shared.
It seems two minutes of her attention
Even now, when the lesson has been learned
Is of more value to you than my years
Of loyal and honest commitment.

5
Last night I dreamed of you.

Last night I dreamed of you
For the first time in an eternity.
Eighteen months to the day
Of your perfidy
You kiss me on the lips as greeting;
I remember how that used to lead to love.
And in the dream I want that one more time
But you will not acquiesce.
You allow me to hold you, in bed, fully clothed
Then you ask me to take you home.
I feel that it is I who am unworthy,
Asking for something I do not deserve,
Feeling ugly as a toad.
Old.
Not good enough for you to love,
For anybody to love.
A very old, very familiar feeling
Not good enough.
Lying lonely in my bed
In my soul.
I have a cat to count on,

He understands loyalty
Even though I give him little time.
My body literally aches
For the connection I had with you
That you severed brutally and suddenly.
I had no clue;
My Father dying in the hospital.
Shortly after your betrayal, he died.
And, I, already bereft from losing you,
Completely fell apart.
Yet it was the pain you caused me
That was overwhelming.
I trusted you.
Next time it will last forever ?
Yet nothing ever lasts in this realm.
Some things are deal breakers,
Sometimes death intervenes.
Love is a scary business.
It can leave you broken on the rocks,
In a cold and unkind sea;
Where you frolicked in the sunshine
Moments earlier.
It can pull you under and leave you breathless,

Where before it held you up to the sun
And you basked in its warmth.
And your love exalted my soul as never before,
Then threw me into the blackest night alone,
With broken life and shattered soul.

6
My Valentines day card.

My Valentines day card
Is the 3 of swords.
The heart in the middle,
Three swords going right through it.
The heartbreak of betrayal
Has kept it pinned in pain a while now.
I cannot entangle myself in love spells any longer
The glamour fades and I sit alone.
Love has never lasted;
One side withers and dies
And poisons the other.
Keep your hearts and flowers,
Your sentimental circus of cliches.
I want none of the illusion.
I will keep my 3 of swords close to my chest,
And have a candlelit dinner with myself.

7

Today I return to the sea.

Today I return to the sea;
Her beautiful wildness inspires me
Untameable, wilful, enthralling
Dancing onto shores all over the world;
The part I see and know and love
Is but a tiny drop
Of the whole goddess.
I stand in her, I swim,
Temporarily become part of her
As I duck under the waves and jump up.
A new baptism,
Into the folds of her arms
And a renewal of my soul
For a new season of my life
I love and revere my sea mother
I worship on her sandy beaches
Her wild winkle lined coves
She is in all life
Bblood is as her salty sentient depths.
We are one.

8
Sea poem...September.

At peace, at ease,
I rise with the swell.
Shells shift, beneath my feet
As I wade deeper,
Into the cold and welcoming water;
Slightly fiercer today ,
Like a cat who wants to play a little rough;
Teasingly scary.
A fairground ride, out of control;
But ultimately holding me safe,
As she tosses me from wave to wave,
Gentle as a featherbed, enveloping;
A lovers embrace.
She knows me almost better
Than I know myself,
Touches all of my hidden secret places;
That only the skilled hand knows.
The sea is my lover, my mother:
The goddess who supports all life
The muse of the deep
Inspiring forever.

You have enchanted
The sea soul deep in my bloodstream.
The mater mari flows both ways.
Always giving and sustaining life;
Holding, embracing,
The touch that takes my breath away!
That every cell of my body is enlivened,
Spoken to in an ancient language
Long forgotten today.
La Ti Fa Tu gently spoken,
La Ti Fa Tu repeated again.
Over my skin,
A benediction;
A sacred sea pledge
That we merge our bodies of water
Once again,
Sensual and deep.....
A feminine union, blessed and divine
We trade wisdom, we commune
She flows into my body cells;
Her electrical, crystalline structure
Fuses with mine
Till I know no longer, where she ends

And I begin.

The secret of the sea

Lives in my bloodline , my soul,

Eternal....

And I always remain true in my promise;

That I will ever return

To perform the sacred,

Sacrosanct, sacrament

Of the secret veil

From whence it all began.

9

The last day by the sea.

The last day by the sea,

Late November.

A year to the day since we buried my Father.

I have grown up a lot in a year.

Shed more tears than I thought possible.

The breach in the walls of my heart still palpable,

I sit on a wall.

The wintry Welsh sea,

A palette of greys, the rocks black;

A sepia scene, set to a misty green wash for hills,

Obscured by rain.

The sand, the warmest kindest colour in the bleakness.

The wind whips my hair around my face.

Again bereft, my aloneness raw

Even nature does not feel to care today;

As I sit, one step removed.

Gone into myself and out of synch.

Today, I am not part of the scene,

A mere alien observer,

In a landscape of a world

I no longer understand.

10

I need to go to the woods.

I need to go to the woods
Where the elementals live;
I need to share my soul
With the frequency of the forest.
I yearn to be part of the natural neural network
Repairing the grid of the planet.
I need to be superconscious;
A connected superconductor
Passing between the worlds,
Speaking to the trees;
The wisdom
Passing to me in a way
I can write it;
To communicate this
To the wider circle of those
On this sacred path;
We heal our souls and remember
What we came here to do.
There are spirits everywhere
In all natural things.
Divine nature beings to work alongside.

We all knew this once
And we have forgotten the sacred.
As we came into cities,
And left nature behind
It receded little by little,
Further and further
Out of our fingertips reach.

We have become disconnected,
And the forest deities
Although content in their tasks,
Miss our company;
Our delight, our news, our human vibration
Between the trees.

Nobody sits and listens
To the wind faeries,
Rustling the leaves,
Asking us to be still and energise from the forces of the forest.
Try sitting barefoot,
Connecting to the earth energies
Ground yourself betwixt the trees,

And listen.

11

To feel what I know.

To feel what I know must proceed.

A whole turn of the cycles,

Processes started, long looming

Before the birth of my earthly ancestors;

Their struggles and pains.

Yet I cannot free them of it

Until we are all free.

The pain upon this world

Is almost unbearable.

Yet we chose to be here.

To bear witness.

As the earth bears down

To give the final pushes.

The birth of a new age.

The past is receding.

The grieving will not last long;

For how long can one cry for despots,

Tyrants and thieves of our birthright

Down the ages?

If we grieve it is for their inabilities.

Their shortcomings.

Devoid and furthermore of nothing
The circle of emptiness embraces them now
With echoes and mirrors of all that they are to focus
upon for an eternity.

Meanwhile, there is a world in turmoil to attend to,.
The howls of anguish
From tortured, brutalized humanity,
Brave, strong, loyal, trusting and BETRAYED.
We know ourselves to be good healers,
With intuitive understanding
Nothing can destroy that spirit,
Over thousands of realms of ages,
Still it triumphs.
Indomitable, wild and free.
United we face the bright new future together.
In memoriam and to the stars,
We did not come here to be on the losing side
Of a bigger battle.
I came, with others, to midwife and safely usher in
the new dawn.
I came to witness all of this unfold,
I came to create a stillness,

A calm

Within the bigger storm that circles around us;

I came with others to calm the frightened,

To soothe and reassure those whose souls are in tatters.

It's alright, my divine mother energy

Harnessed to its full potential,

Can heal multitudes.

It takes very little really

To have an extensive reach.

And a small amount of love,

Amplifies on its journey

To any and all who need it.

Agape the Greeks called it,

We have lost the definition here;

Our language confused and infantilised,

A basic babble of vocabulary

Where once was sophisticated language

Thoughts and thinking.

Education trained the soul

To the things of the higher mind.

Culture, philosophy, grammar and rhetoric.

This time the baby will not be stillborn.

This is the time that was long foretold
That humanity throws off its chains
Stands together in unity and brotherhood.
We are here to witness the achievement,
The evolution and to share with them
In celebration and heartfelt joy.

12

We know so little of our earth lineages

We know so little of our earth lineages
Yet my father invited me here.
He sought a daughter in his image
And here I am. I continue his work.
Being a woman I work differently,
I can be more overt, more rebellious.
Have an impact on more people unnoticed.
It is a great strength to be female in a dying patriarchy.
It is a serious and solemn calling.
I'm here but parts of me are not of, or from, here.
I remember this more and more.
I'm biding my time in the shadows.
Learning and remembering the wisdom
That the evildoers wish we would forget.
They try to breathe the dust of death
Upon a mighty and noble race.
There have been many genocides.
Burnings of books and "Heretics",
Those with sufficient strength of spirit to resist.

These are our heroes and exemplars.
Those who cannot be bought at any price
Payable on this rotten and perished system.
I'm not from here.
I know.
It needs to be my secret.
I work unnoticed in the shadows,
Where no profits are turned,
Where my colleagues are as am I.
I am come to find my tribe
I am privileged to be among my kin;
I can work with my passion
And be paid enough to pay my bills.
I am fortunate indeed
To be trusted with a position
Of influence here where there are truths.
Human stories, human souls
Not all of earthly origin,
Who have failed to thrive here.
We nurture and care for them.
It is a sacred duty.
I pray I may never lose sight of this.
For it is my calling.

To learn, to be accepted
To be part of a guild of humanity.
For in helping today's vulnerable
I am assisting my ancestors
Through these works of service.
Each human being suffering, is a god.
Our job is to teach them
As children how to understand
How to temper those basic emotions
Into the finest crafted swords
That we can brandish.
Coming out of the shadows
Standing strong to reclaim our freedom
For all time.
I bring my skills of womanly wisdom
Healing and understanding to the fore.
So long it has been unacknowledged
Given freely for no thanks
Yet it has poured a smooth riverbed
Over which the waters of my children's lives
Flow peacefully for the most part.
This is the path to my souls growth.
A collection of new life stories to learn,

New journeys touching paths with others
To smooth our way.

13
I need grounding.

I need grounding.

It is so many days since my bare feet made touch,

Electrical piezoelectric contact

With the sacred earth.

Planting my etheric roots,

Far, far, down into the inner layers.

Exchanging energy and information

Through threads of yellows and oranges,

With red disc like nodes;

That penetrate down into the dark brown,

Warm loamy love and heart warmth,

Emanating from the deepest

Sacredness of the womb of the Goddess.

Once again, I am reminded

Of the time when I was oh so lost.

Adrift in the sacred space;

That from afar had seemed cold, black, empty;

Yet was suffused with warmth, love

And utter benevolence and care

Experienced rarely by mere mortals,

Except when in those points of extremis

Where there is nothing left to do
But let go completely.
For all that I held fast upon
Unravelled faster than ancient threads,
Until I held only dust in my hands.
You nurture me now
As you cradled me then.
Dependable, tireless, timeless as oceans,
As aeons.
And do I trust you beyond all others
My dearest Goddess ?
Why of course, for you were always there
Omnipresent.
When the cells fused that formed my being,
In the creative, starlit, fertile void
From whence all begins and returns.
I sense the truth in all matters
In the central space within me;
Wherein all that is real is discern'ed,
Truth weighed and sifted from falsehood.
My whole being is so much more tuned in
Since my souls sweet surrender.
I trust,

I feel,
I believe.
All will be more than well.
For the plan itself, born in the purest of hearts
Is perfection absolute.
The trees tell me to stand firm.
Nurturing myself in the earth's warm energy
As I feel it being drawn up.
Through the soles of my feet,
Through my body it surges,
Lively as spring;
Through every fibre of my being,
Up and out through my fingertips,
Channeled via every strand of my hair,
And passed outwards into my auric shield.
Sprinkling love and goodwill into the world about me
With every intentioned step.
I remember always to reconnect.
In it lies my fulfillment
And the source of my power
To change the world.

14

I only got here yesterday.

I only got here yesterday

And spent one night.

The silence is beautiful,

The solitude feels like a guilty pleasure.

I need this.

I need enough of this that I feel mended,

That I get to where I need to be,

And feel that I am enough

That all my strivings are not in vain.

That I find peace of mind;

In this battle pocked hellhole of a world.

I'm traumatised as we all are

By the conditions I see in the globe

But not in my personal life.

I am privileged in so far as to have a tolerable life

If it is not exactly easy.

My biggest difficulty is that

I need to do this regularly.

To decompress and relax,

To remember who I am ,

And to triage my wounds

With soothing silence
Out of survival mode
A few brief days.
This is my lifeline
The part I need to keep myself together
Amidst the madness
Of the system I have to live within.
It takes all my energy ordinarily
And I can never find enough silence;
Enough alone time,
Where nobody will bother me.
My phone is in another room, no wifi
I can do as I wish here.
Moment to moment I feel a peace
And a freedom that I can never find
In the city.
Which intimidates and scares me.
A completely other set of principles to my own values.
The law of the soulless, the selfish, the greedy
Unaware of any realm
But the grim grey streets
And the drab clothes they wear.

Everyone is an object
To use as you will.
No compassion,
No sensitivity or emotions,
For they have none
And as I cannot play that game
Nor wish to,
I will keep my distance.

15

Sing back life into the sacred sites.

Sing back life into the sacred sites,
The well nymphs grow sad in silence.
A locked door prevents
Their magical communion with mankind.
They miss our company, our news,
They miss our songs.
The counterpoint and harmony to their own
Which vibrates a resonance -
In tune with nature,
Bringing us back into balance
Returning us home to our souls.
Nymphs of sacred spaces;
My heart abides with you
We have no stake in the world of men.
I Reconnect, I sing at sacred sites
I connect us back to the nodes of nature
With healing crystals, shells and stones.
I sing to you nature spirits of the well
I know you hear and reside around this sacred space;
From the depths where you are entombed
Cut off from me as I am from you,

So I reach through the bars of the drab painted door.
Our hands reach across the barriers and dimensions
And we entwine our fingers and exchange the knowledge
Of all that we are.
I leave shells for you.
A reminder of the nearby sea.
A gift I give infused with my love,
And all that I know of life in this world
Outside of the peace of the well
That I cannot access and you cannot escape.
We are twins across a firmament
Neither can overcome.
Yet our awareness of each other;
Our touching of hands,
Passes on the understanding we both need at this time.
I love you nature spirits and elementals.
I reach you with my compassion
And with your etheric touch I feel you.
Deep in my heart I feel the sadness
Of our imbalanced existence in an artificial world.

To you I give flowers, crystals, silver coins and shells.
To myself the remembrance that we are one.
Completion.

16

Every sacred forest.

Every sacred forest,(Every forest is sacred)
Has at it's heart a mighty ancient oak.
It IS the heart of the forest:
Holding all the wisdom, understanding and balance
Of the entire system.
The ancient tree is the King of the forest kingdom,
Hearing all the sounds and thoughts of all others,
And keeping all in balance, safe from harm.
Sending out antibodies towards infections
The cog at the middle of the clock of the cosmos.
The whole forest is in communication with itself
All it is, an entirety in and of itself.
When a patch is destroyed
It is as if a limb has been cut off.
It traumatises the earth and the other entities.
The heart of the forest, works on
Through the seasons, days and nights,
Maintaining balance and a safe space
For humankind to retreat into
And learn of the ways of nature.
The sacred old ways many of us lost

Yet which remain in the hearts and souls of the old ones.
Those who have never forgotten the bond and reverence
Between people and the sacredness of the forest.

17
The trees are sleeping.

The trees are sleeping,
Storing their resources.
Saving their prana
For the right moment
To shoot forth life,
From delicate branches
That point upwards like fingertips,
Eager to catch the sunlight.

There are no masters or controllers
in the forest.
The trees do not need a uniformed fool
To tell them when to bring forth blossom,
When to drop the connection to the leaves
And to rest.

The fool would tell the tree to bud
Blossom and fruit all the time.
Never to rest, pause or reflect;
Never to take time to breathe and just be.
The trees are old and have many memories

They see uniformed fools come and go
And still they stand in their glory.
Rooted in their sovereignty
Unhurried, unbothered by the follies of men
They watch, they know, they record all
In their long memories,
They exchange information across the ether
Faster than the internet.
Their group consciousness
Knows more than TV news,
And they stand proud.
Waiting,
Watching incredible things unroll,
At this important point in time.
And here are we two,
Standing in the forest,
Communing with the trees,
The nature spirits, the consciousness
And where we are absolutely welcomed
In our conscious intention to connect.

18
I dive deep

I dive deep

Into the stream of cosmic consciousness.

Down through the shallow layers,

Into the sparkling stardust depths,

To bring you a pearl.

A hidden treasure

From the deepest cave.

There is no point in finding treasure

If one is merely to sit upon it

And hide it away from the world.

For it must be burnished by the light of truth.

And held aloft that all should see it.

A witness to higher things occurring

Beneath the tawdry lacquer on the world.

Things are moving, shifting, in a way

That has not been seen before.

Here, in this day we currently inhabit,

This transitory, transitional, liminal space

Is formed the new world.

We step forward in confidence,

With optimism and healing.

Cleansed of all the dreadful facts
That had to be heard to proceed.
The dirty underbelly of the sick,
Corrosive, rotting, evil, beast system
Unsettled and devastated us
That these things went unpunished,
Unseen for so very very long.
That it took trauma on this scale,
Our people had to see such filth
To fully understand.
That we dealt not with principalities
But an older much greater evil,
Ancient and well versed in all aspects
Of running a slavery system.
Whose plans to do so here,
Only faltered and fell apart,
When they got too greedy,
Pushed too hard too fast,
And were consumed by their own
Hubristic darkness.
They are gone, it is done.
Here we begin to clear up the darkness,
Tend to the wounded and know

That such gargantuan gaslighting
Will never happen again.
And that we know better
However, I see myself writing this
A long time before. At another fall.
We never really thought they would
Infiltrate and destroy our world.
We realised too late their malign hearts
And somehow they overtook us.
We have spent 12,000 years in the wilderness
Recovering, remembering, healing,
Growing stronger,
While the same evil ones tightened their control
Over the new world that they had created in their distorted image.
Empires and tyranny dominated,
As they fashioned the apparatus
For their false idols and techno gods.
Using the resources of the whole world,
To create a technologically superior,
Yet spiritually bankrupt negatively oriented society,
Where inverted souls prosper,
And integrity is sneered upon.

This is finished.
This is done.
In finality and eternity.
We stand sovereign as one.
And withdraw all the consent,
That was wrongfully and deceptively
Stolen from us.
The cheating legalese system
And the monetary slavery system is fallen.
The great whore of Babylon
Is fallen from her throne,
Her effigy of gold has toppled -
The head is broken off now.
People rejoice in the streets at her death,
Her unrighteous wrongdoings
Have left her undone.
Justice is served by lady liberty
No longer looking at the sunrise of the evil empire,
But at the brightest sun,
Which burned away the dross;
Brought all truth into clear focus
And heralded the real new day.
No longer an ersatz overlay

Of deception or fear,

For it could not withstand the light of truth.

We stand as one. We stand taller.

A race who found their voice,

Their righteous anger,

Their commitment to stand firm

In the face of seemingly overwhelming opposition.

We are powerful beyond belief,

And what we visualise we create,

For we are the gods. A part of the sphere.

The multifaceted whole of which each is a lens;

A feed into the creation of the story,

That we write on the vellum of our world.

We no longer create the will of tyrants

No longer in the bondage of fear.

Our creative potential is free.

Working on solving of problems

Created by a small contemptuous hive mind

Powered only by our goodwill.

Once we withdrew our energy,

It withered, fizzled and died

And they went with it.

Into the void.

Where they will finally be dealt with
As they so richly deserve.

19
A black rock.

A black rock.

Smooth and full of mystery

On a Devon beach.

Maybe it is a piece of meteorite,

Fallen from far flung spaces in the past and future simultaneously,

Outside of this beautiful blue green bauble.

Tiny in size but unique in all the galaxies.

Time irrelevant, time immemorial,

Time the stone by which we tarry and to which we are bound.

The sacrifice as we are born, grow, sicken and die,

Over and over.

Endless repeating patterns,

Yet how forgetful we are.

Standing on the shore,

Dipping our toes into the memories,

Of lifetimes and cycles that we know innately

Yet have forgotten in our physical cognition.

Take my hand, let us ride the winds of time

Back and forwards swirling through colour and

clouds,

Onwards, upwards to a different place

That we once knew so well.

20
I sit on the back of the eagle.

I sit on the back of the eagle.
He flies high above rainforests,
Rivers, deserts, the Grand Canyon.
He is huge and I hold onto his body.
Sat between his wings,
He tells me telepathically
How all this has been here for such a long time,
And lots of different people have come and gone
Over long millennia,
Yet this generation is the most lost,
Most disconnected, least understanding
Of our roles as protectors and listeners,
Of the wisdom of the natural places,
Of their healing energies,
And of what they can teach us.
How we need to work together in harmony,
And that the animals and plants,
Will share with us
Their wisdoms and truths,
How the spirit extant in all of nature
Seeks to offer solace and support,

Unconditional love and acceptance,
To the pure of heart who wish to do no harm.
As he flies in the sunshine
With me on his back,
I feel his warmth, his feathers, his energy
I feel so connected that I forget I ever felt lonely,
Isolated, friendless and without love at all.
He understands my every thought,
My heart and soul.
All living things can do this,
We are from the same creative source after all.
We are atoms of the same molecules,
Dancing around the centre pole of the galaxy.
All is one,
The patterning from the smallest to the biggest.
Under the earth, up to the vastnesses of space,
The mechanisms and natural laws are all the same
From any perspective.
And having shown me all of this,
Grandfather Eagle sets me down gently, safely,
Once again, and I hug him, giving thanks
For all that he has shared with me
As we take off back to our own worlds.

He to the skies, and I, to a quiet place to write
And ponder on this great gift of understanding
He has given me.

21

I love Cornwall.

I love Cornwall.

The peaceful place,

The crowsong outside my window.

The knowledgeable trees,

And remnants of my ancestors memories.

The Celts,

Their culture is still alive here.

Untrampled by the Roman sandals,

That imprinted the rest of the country,

With their values and words

That are still clear a couple of thousands of years hence,

Down here there are plenty of places

That still ring with the tones

Of a now lost language;

Where Neolithic relics still stand

In the weatherbeaten landscapes.

Here the energy is still pure,

The old ways are still followed.

Here I can be my authentic self,

Grounding myself among Merry Maidens

In remembrance of a lost friend
Who once came here and healed the stones;
Reconnecting them to the grid
Disrupted long ago.
There is peace, safety and no pressure here.
No responsibility save for myself.
Nobody to answer to or attend to.
I am by myself
I finally feel relaxed, off duty
Calm and at peace,
Free to do as I wish.
Which is to reconnect myself,
Once again with my divine mother,
The earth consciousness.

22

Waiting for the rain.

We need the rain.

The clouds hover grey and brooding

Yet nothing falls.

We take refuge in the greenhouse,

Awaiting the first drops.

Picnic plates all cleared away,

Newly planted marigolds gasping for the

Life giving drops to quench the soil.

We sit on battered leather armchairs

Tired and content..

A long walk, a pleasant lunch.

At the river we were gifted

With the vision of a kingfisher.

Blue and golden jewel;

Vibrant as a hummingbird

He flashed down onto the river

Catching silver fish that sparkled in the sun

As they twisted in the pointed beak.

The first few drops fall.

Tapping on the glass panes

Like babies fingers, gently.

Hesitant, we sit. And wait

For the deluge.

The thunder and lightning storm

We feel in our fingers

Is waiting.

The rain is harder now

Tears running down the glass,

The tapping harder.

Talking to our heartbeats

Of the untameable power

Of nature and of our human spirits.

We sit still in the centre of the storm,

Enjoying the wild elements

From this vantage point

At the centre of our world.

23

There's a massive shifting going on.

There's a massive shifting going on.
It's irresistible. It will not be stopped.
The time of the harvest is approaching.
Those who can raise their consciousness
And vibration, and who care
For humanity and all in creation,
From the smallest microbe,
To the biggest supernova.
Those who understand the interconnected nature
Of all we are and all we survey,
And all that is unseen
Except with ancient inner senses.
Those who take seriously
The life they are living here,
And remember a time before time
In a deep and ancient part of their soul.
Those who reconnect the energies,
Talk to the spirits of nature
And understand the language of the cosmos.
The wild world is calling us to it;
To raise the frequency

To stir the stagnant energy,
To take our place once more,
Where we belong, among the stars;
With benign dominion over creation.
Our hearts to lead the way.
We are so powerful,
Beyond what we have dared to imagine.
And it is time to step
Fully into our power, our sovereignty
And change the pattern forever.

24

I am in love with the world.

I am in love with the world.
The natural spirits move my soul.
I fly with the ravens,
Wriggle my toes in the soil with the worms and centipedes.
I swim in the living sea with the fishes,
And breathe in the life force
Freely available everywhere I am.
I feel more deeply by the day.
My heart expands ever further,
Drawing compassionate others
Closer into my trajectory.
The plants whisper and rustle-
Each a unique individual
In a group of souls.
I spend so long in the greenery
That I connect roots;
Leaves and branches
Onto my intuitive aerials,
And reach out deeper into the woodland.
Placing crystals, doubling the power

On energy lines.
I am tuning further in
Alongside another of the same soul.
The power is amplified again.
Ancient memories now begin to manifest.
Deep in my core.
I feel alive in every cell,
Every filament of my electrical being
Tingles with excitement,
For the great work
I have become immersed in,
Here on the beautiful blue and green planet,
Terra, that I have sometimes called home.
My future and past selves
Are here joined together.
Simultaneously reaching forwards and backwards
To my current incarnation.
A shiver down my spine
Confirms this to be truth.
I need no outside validation.
With sacred masculine beside me.
We complete a circuit, a quartz crystal-
An old yew on an energy node

Our subtle energies combine.

We heal the gridlines

And recharge what was forgotten,

Thought to have been long lost.

As we journey together,

Home to awareness

Of our eternal selves,

For a few brief years in a lifetime already more than half over,

But connected to all that is

And has ever been.

All that we are....

A small part of the whole,

Stitched back together

Against the patchwork colours

Of earth and sky.

25

The bond a woman may have with a cat.

The bond a woman may have with a cat

Is strong and deep.

I communicate with mine

With eye gazing and blinks,

Murmured mews and purring.

I love to gaze on him when he is sleeping,

This wild creature with a love of soft furnishings!

Sometimes he play-fights me,

Purring all the while

As he nibbles and licks my hand,

Holding my wrists with his clawed white gloves,

But oh so subtly !

He still has his wildness,

As I still have mine.

A graceful blending with nature.

My bond with my cat,

Brings me into balance with the outdoors.

He is the conduit that brings natures energy,

Uncontaminated and pure into my heart.

He renews my faith in the world,
And is soothing to my soul.
He is a walker between the three worlds.
Of nature, people and the spirit realm he sees
With his enhanced perception.
He chases away harm in many guises.
He may look physically small and ineffectual
But to believe that is to underestimate both of us.
Just a woman and her cat,
Working together in peace and harmony
Since forever.

26

I'm a lone witch walking.

I'm a lone witch walking,
Stubborn and strong.
Following my nature
And not the rules of men.
I'm independent and in love with myself now
For the others to whom I gave my heart
Failed in one way or another to be as true.
I trust myself. So could they
But held their authentic selves back
Maybe unaware, maybe selfishly
Giving the smallest crumbs they could
While enjoying the banquet I prepared for them.
I made them feel special
They were the centre of the world
And I was there to attend to the details.

I know there are some amazing sacred men.
I have met them.
They are usually married to wonderful women.
There is no struggle or issue they cannot solve.
Working together in harmony.

The attributes of the one,

Blending with the qualities of the other.

To create a strength and unity that can pass any test.

Total trust and honesty, openness of heart and soul

The foundation of the house.

This is the only type of relationship

Worth having.

27

I've always loved to write.

I've always loved to write,
Inspiration has come to me
Throughout my life.
The delicious ideas,
That come along with home made cake
At Sue's cottage sustained me,
In days when not much time was my own.
Recognition, like the picture postcards
We used as prompts one day
Was freeing.
Allowing myself to soar above
The branches and into the sky,
It felt so liberating !
My need to communicate
Recognised and validated at last.
Sue now runs a creative café on the coast
And my life too is transformed,
But I fondly remember the days
We spent in creative reverie
That now seem so long ago.

28

There's a very fine line

There's a very fine line
Twixt wisdom and folly,
Crazy and sainted.
Listening to the inner soul.
One has no need of teachers,
For all is available in my experience.
I am and I have all that I need.
Always I will have enough
To carry me forward,
To bring others with me,
And unlock the secrets of
More hearts and souls.
All in my life
Is mine own experience;
All are different.
Paths and lifescripts
Set in motion long ago.
I go with the flow,
Listen to my inner urgings,
There's something urging me
To an ancient place,

Of what does it seek to remind me?

29

I'm the kind of woman.

I'm the kind of woman
Whose soul wanders around,
And has full freedom to take me where it will.
I am attuning to the ease
That comes with letting go
Of any illusion of control,
Or need to try to control
Any aspect of my life.
A tricky concept.
There are times we need to act and take action
But can we really control anything here?
Love and death show us otherwise
We have no choice over who we love,
The passion that ignites with only a few other souls in any lifetime.
The control lies only in choosing
To stay or walk away,
From any particular lesson
And to choose a different one.
We always know exactly where to go in life
If we only listen inwards.

If we do our best and are sincere
We will not go far wrong.
Even bad decisions yield fruit,
The fools folly becomes the sages wisdom.
Transmutation achieved over a lifetime.
I was a strange child
Always wanting to understand, asking questions;
People baffled me so -
Seemed to speak unspoken language that I could not grasp,
And I struggled to learn it.
In middle age I can do it a bit.
But I still end up blurting something real,
Sometimes it is reciprocated with authenticity,
A glimpse behind the veil to the pure unguarded soul
That revels in its uniqueness.
Exchanging the strange with strangers
Is an excellent pastime sometimes.
Most rewarding.
I wonder if everyone is secretly as strange as me
But so much better at hiding it?
Do others have random thoughts
That wander a myriad of paths

To explore further avenues of knowledge?
I need to learn as much as I can
About as many things as I can
And now is the time to be myself,
Plant seeds and see what grows……..

30
On the day of a funeral

On the occasion of a funeral
To have a catch up with an old friend
Unexpectedly seen at a funeral
Was an enriching experience.
We spoke of mutual friends
Our life experiences
And the Mandela effect.
He is a rational atheist
And I was pleased to find
That my views on spirituality
And his on physics
Held a lot more common ground
Than either of us would have thought.
We spoke of parallel universes overlapping;
Timelines being crossed, translocation
And the 5th density.
Whether the universe is created from pure consciousness,
And if we are role players in a cosmic game
Having chosen to put on a meatsuit
To experience life on a denser planet

To taste, to touch, to make a difference
Or for a vacation.
Who really knows the answers ?

31

In a past life regression.

In a past life regression

I was a Celtic man with long hair

A grey kilt and roman sandals.

I worked in the forests.

I had a beautiful wife

With long dark hair,

Who loved me deeply

Gave me two small boys.

She was slender and tall.

One day I came home from my work,

And my family were gone.

Our house was on fire.

I howled in despair, sat down and cried.

My life destroyed.

32
Disconnecting from the cogs and gears.

Disconnecting from the cogs and gears;
The traps and snares of the tricky, monkey, ego mind,
I can focus on the divine.
The brute still sticks up his ugly head,
Chattering away,
Demanding to be heard;
And I tell him he is an irrelevance:
An outmoded way of archontic thinking,
A mind I never agreed to be given,
That causes nothing but trouble,
For it is primitive, and as such
Sees the world as I increasingly do not.
For a long while it was who I thought I was.
In the beginning when I knew no better,
In a world built to pander to its urges.
Materialistic, acquisitive, ever hungry
But never satisfied,
Filling me with doubts.
Whispering criticisms in my ear,

In control.
However it is not me.
I am the softer, tactile, warm being
Who resides further down.
Beyond the head's programmes,
A deep and rich seam of wisdom,
Molten and golden burns in my soul,
And I am able to tune in, and listen
To an entirely different voice.
Supportive and understanding,
With the answers to anything in the whole universe
that I may ponder.
This is the part not moved by gewgaws
Or trifles or petty spite.
This is my true self.
Old as the mountains,
Sparking as stardust
It is my guide, my golden compass.
I need have no plans, no worries,
For I am ever guided and need none.
I cannot put a foot wrong on this path,
For I see only that I need.
The next step.

I am guided by the entire wisdom
Of eternity collated from forever....
From every source, experience, lifetime;
And therefore I need naught else.
Nobody to tell me what I should do.
I am here and that's enough.
If I look, I can find old memories;
From places I have never taken this body.
Small, fractal, fragments of the past.
Uncovered as and when there is something I need to know.
To help me.
I have no fear of death
For I am eternal, powerful and loved.
And I have never been alone.

33
I do not bathe every day.

I do not bathe every day, although many do,
I remember tens of lives
Where running water was a luxury
And a hot clean bath was rare.
I do not need to do this every day
My body is not overly sweaty or greasy,
And I enjoy the sense of occasion
When I sink into a long,deep candlelit sea salt bath
And consider my ancestors,
The ease of my life in comparison with theirs.
I have no complaints about my small elderly car,
My soft bed, my physically undemanding job.
Yet I lack a community,
A common cause with others.
No connection, it being broken
By television long before I came along.
The digital overlay on reality
Shaping expectations and social change:
A rebellious revolution,
And new generations, who absorb
The latest messages of the paradigm

And deem previous generations out of touch,
Their experiences and wisdom of no value,
Because this is the "now" generation.
Selfish, individualistic, egotistical, hedonistic,
All instant gratification and entitlement,
Standing on the rapidly shifting sands
Of "opinion formers"
Keep up quick, or become obsolete
Be left behind, …Oh the horror
Of not having the latest tech gadget
The most up to date phone or Tv…!
They really believe that today's world
Is the zenith of civilisation
When it is actually reaching it's nadir.
People stopped listening to their elders long ago.
Instead we have youth culture, vapid, superficial, materialistic.
Buy it while its hot!
While you are young and gullible,
While you think it has the answers
That the influencers have some wisdom.
Before the truth sinks in and you realise
You have spent your time

Buying a personality off the peg,
From one of the system's approved boutiques
And become a caricature, a stereotype,
With everything money can buy
But there's still a hole, unfillable,
With objects or money,
That howls from the void inside
That this is not enough.
The hole is programmed in,
And we are told that we can buy fulfilment.
But objects and money can never replace
Connection, intimacy, kindness, nature, truth, trust,
love and freedom.
These things are simple but they're free.
We have been indoctrinated;
A species with amnesia.
We are so tangled up in deceptions
About ourselves as well as all else,
That it takes considerable effort to remember,
And be rooted back into our authentic selves
But that is the only way
To fill the void.

34

I spend so little time alone.

I spend so little time alone,
Yet I prefer it to the company of most people.
What can you offer me
That can match my solitude ?
My peace of mind in the silence ?
Just the slow steady staccato tick of the clock
As I dissolve back into my true self
And enjoy the freedom from all expectation
All duty, all day.
I would love to have a soundproof room
To relax in, when I choose,
Rather than waiting for a quiet house.
And no neighbours moving or banging
Or grinding metal or dogs barking
Or people talking, even with the window shut
I can hear every banal word.
This is my time and my space,
And I pursue it like a suitor
Eagerly awaiting it's tender tendril embrace once again.
It feels illicit, somehow wrong

To enjoy my own company so much.
To spend time with stillness, my secret lover !

35

The wheel turns to the autumn equinox.

The wheel turns to the autumn equinox,
The harvest is in, the stubble burned
As the sun moves further away,
Or rather we tip away from the golden sphere
That provides sustenance to all life here,
And the other hemisphere gets the kiss of warmth
While we grow colder,
The light watery on a misty morning walk.

Someone once told me
That the planets used to be in perfect harmony,
Before the cataclysm that knocked them
All off centre and created seasons.
That we lived in Elysian fields,
And the whole planet had a temperate temperature
All year round, with plentiful food
Abundance for all, and a deep respect for all humanity
Then revered as the divine sovereign beings we are

And in touch with the living Earth.

Where women's quiet wisdom healing and creative endeavours
Were as admired as the activities of menfolk,
And there were no hierarchies;
Save that those who lived in service to others
And respected the higher natural laws
Were held in the highest esteem;
And even grew more physically beautiful
In accordance with their souls evolution.

This of course occurred
Before the fall in consciousness,
That led us into the dark abysmal world
We now inhabit, as royalty yoked as slaves;
Chained to the demiurge's desperate, degenerate system,
Oppression and inversion, materialistic depravity
No longer free or sovereign,
In their system of servitude.
To their impotent angry gods,
Of power, wealth and inequality,

Who care nothing for nobility of spirit;
For they have no such trait,
Seeing only a naked dollar sign
On every divine living thing on the planet.
Morally and spiritually bankrupt
And so jealous it's untrue.
Ever fearful their dirty souls will be brought into the light
For all to see.

36
Samhain.

Samhain

Time of the ancestors.

I cook a traditional stew from scratch,

And consider the generations who came before me,

Their genes still twinkling in my eyes.

I don't know them but there is a familiarity.

I feel them around me in my kitchen

As I prepare shallots and swedes;

Chunks of lamb and woodland mushrooms.

I consider previous generations doing the same things

Their lives in different times.

My life seems easy compared to the older ones,

I have hot water, a comfy bed,

A machine that washes and wrings out my laundry,

A warm house in the winter,

I live in a world where I could travel anywhere,

I have a world of information and music at my fingertips

Yet for all of this,

The sense of community,

Of connection to others is missing.
I am isolated, in my draughtproof dwelling,
Looking outwards as I wonder how the others
Are so easily entertained with the banal,
Having lost their place in time and space here.

I carry forward the torch now,
Without my forbears I would not be here.
Yet they would be horrified at how a life of ease
Has made a whole generation, soft, unskilled, half alive.
Even I, grasping around the outermost edges of healing and magic
Have a lot to learn,
And even more to remember
As I take my place in the line.
I have continued the mother line another two generations
With daughters and granddaughters;
Once my mother is gone I will be the next to slip into the past
And join the line that stretches into forever.
Having bequeathed all of the wisdom

I have been able to collect up

From the scattered edges of my world,

The breadcrumbs that I, hunter gatherer, seek

And hold in my skirts,

Keep safe to pass on

In song and story.

Preserving the magic

Another spread of years

In remembrance

In an ever-changing world.

Twas ever thus.

37

I'm finding my tribe now.

I'm finding my tribe now.

I walk alone, I always did,

I prefer solitude to tedious company,

To compromise, to time wasting pursuits.

I'm here to learn and help,

Not necessarily to be liked.

Always the outsider

I realise now it is because I see

Clearly from outside,

Objective and true.

I can think with clarity,

Trust myself

Go whither I will

At the drop of a hat

A moment's notice.

I roam free,

Lots of things catch my fascination.

On this path, I'm learning fast.

Sometimes relearning things that I had lost.

Realising all of the important things,

Are felt and known in heart and soul,
Much more than the head.
Truth is deep within,
And we have strayed so far away
From nature, the angels,
And our truest selves
That we need reminding.
Be still …..and know.
Learn to listen,
For in the small silence
There are great visions to be seen.
Deep within, beautifully coloured meaningful images,
Containing a wealth and depth of meaning.
Go deeper…..
What do you need to know?
How to best listen to our intuition?
To witness the process of our transformation
From the basest clay Caliban
To the airy sprite;
We hover betwixt
Yet can aspire to either
In each incarnation
On this most beautiful of worlds.

38

The total silence of a quiet house.

The total silence of a quiet house.
They've all gone out except the cat.
He relaxes, twitching in his sleep
By my side on my bedcovers.
I love silence, peace and quiet,
I savour it like a fine morsel
Or a full bodied vintage red.
The stillness of no bustling activity.
No clanging in the kitchen,
No trips to the loo next door
In my own space, my energy
Can spread to fill the entire space
No one else around,
I sit propped up on pillows in bed
With a strong black coffee,
And a bowl of caramel latte ice cream
Perfected with a big blob of clotted cream,
A sprinkling of coffee granules
And a dusting of desiccated coconut and flaked almonds
I am grateful for the relaxation I enjoy,

And already dreading its loss once again.

39

I was a lone witch walking.

I was a lone witch walking

By myself among the trees,

In nature where I fit best.

Now with a kindred grandchild in tow.

Her blue eyes look in wonder

At all she surveys,

Captivated by the novelty of Earth life.

A perfect human child;

Untainted as yet by walking the wires of the overlay,

Still fresh and hopeful as she came,

Through the portal within her Mother

Where grew her body;

Though not her soul which may well be older than mine…

The keys to our original relationship

May or may not ever be seen here.

She looks at a woodlouse, a snail, a spider's web,

A vine snaking up a tree.

"Wow" she says in awe

 At the small miracles of the natural world,

And grounds me back again

Into the wonder.

My own reasons for embarking on this journey.

Long ago, in another place

I came to experience this beautiful planet,

Yet whose ways I do not really understand.

The child who walks with me,

And the child who walks within me,

Are however perfectly aligned

We hold hands, look into each other's souls,

And smile,

As she leads me off

Deeper into the woods and my soul memories

To further wondrous discoveries

As the birds sing, the sun shines,

And the energy of the ancient forest

Dances with imagination and magic.

40

The company of women.

The company of women,
Is something I had little experience of
Until very recently.
I was wary having had experience
Of backstabbers, blabbers and gossips.
I had found occasional women trustworthy,
But in general I found we had nothing in common.
Communication was confusing,
Games were played, and I came off worst;
The victim of bullies and gossips.
My openness held against me,
In a shady shielded world
Where I didn't know the rules
Now that I am older I understand
The people around me were wrong
And that to live an authentic life,
One is to be as I was all along,
Once the fear of judgement of others is gone,
Freedom follows.
To come to the point of giving no fucks,
To be real,

And have no fear of the consequences
Is the most powerful of positions and liberating.
All of the energy previously spent worrying is gone forever.
To be used constructively on whatever I choose.
Learning new skills, feeling truly empowered
For the first time.
Having a circle of women I can trust,
Who do not pass judgement on each other,
Who understand the world as I do,
Who are kind and generous,
With compliments, afternoon tea,
And clothes swaps at each others homes,
We are the connections of the world.

41

I trust a circle of women.

I trust a circle of women;

Kind and supportive

Who give their time and energy freely

And the exchange is equal.

We have learned to love ourselves

And take care of each other.

There is kindness and honour

Trust and integrity,

Generosity and warmth

We are real, we are open

We are unafraid of judgement.

We are outspoken, we tell the truth

And we do not respect the "man" archy

In its biggest or smallest manifestations;

In fact we see how ridiculous it all is

And sometimes (but don't tell anyone !)

We roar with laughter

At the idea that men think

They can control our subversive thoughts

As easily as they have controlled our physical reality.

They are right to suspect that we laugh at them

But that is no reason to kill us.
This is the reason that certain types of men
Have always felt threatened
By women spending time together in groups without them.
We realise the truth and stop co-operating.
We reclaim our power,
And leave them to their own menial tasks
While we live free of slavery;
In a community of lovely, lively, happy ,
Strong, rebellious women who know the truth.

42

The media tells older women.

The media tells older women

That we are no longer of value.

Though older and wiser,

Filled with knowledge

We are no longer comely, biddable.

No longer easily manipulated.

Long ago were we maidens;

With youth,

And beauty,

And gullibility.

Able to be seduced and harmed

By insincere men

With flattery and bullshit.

Worthless baubles.

Now,

Having lost our market value

No longer naive to their deceptions

No longer young and fuckable,

We are ignored,

Except by those who truly see us

As entire people,

And love us for our skills, souls and inner qualities

Which after all are what endure.

We are the crone.

Despised and feared.

In days gone by,

Older women were respected.

All of our wisdom

From decades of life;

From having dominion

Over the sacred portals

Of life and death ;

Of healing as of blessing,

Of empathy and listening,

Sound advice and guidance,

Has been devalued.

By the narcissistic cult of youth,

Which values only the new;

The bright and shiny,

Superficial and material,

Hypersexual or highly technical.

Shallow meaningless pastimes,

Dehumanising transhumanist ideals,

Downmarket morals in the tabloids

Reality TV shows
Where ignorance is applauded,
Debauchery celebrated,
And erroneous thinking rewarded.
Far away from the past lives we remember
Our goddess energy now seen as irrelevant.
In a world where appearance is all.
I enjoy my anonymity .
After a lifetime not being taken seriously,
My opinion not considered of any consequence
Among the discourse of men,
To be spoken to but never heard,
I can hide in plain sight these days.
Keeping my wisdom to myself.
How sad that men are considered to have
Greater gravitas the older they get,
Even when they are pompous fools!
Yet women, the keepers of the flame,
The guardians of the heart energy of the world;
Are undervalued.
A disposable commodity
Whose time and energy,
Caring and patience,

Is expected to be expended forever
For no thanks or reward.
We are the keepers of the flame
And some of us still remember.
We may be isolated here and there
In ones or twos who keep the knowing.
Yet our time is coming.
When all the irrelevance falls away
Falls apart, as it will very soon,
When the truth comes out,
in all its horrific forms;
It will be to us that the people return,
And we will be set in our rightful position
Once more regarded as wise and benevolent,
The mature facet of the goddess energy.
The one who guards and protects all others,
With our fierce passion for justice,
In our expansive arms,
Against our soft bosom
We shall embrace all of the people of the world,
Washing them clean of illusion
In remembrance once again.
For they are our people

And hold the blueprint
Of the divine energy that we are.

43

On Women's Day.

On Women's Day,
I give thanks
For the power of women,
The solidarity of sisterhood.
The special energy
That exists in an all female group,
In deep trust and sacred respect,
For our common experiences.
Walking representatives
Of the divine feminine
In the world.
We accomplish much quietly
Without recognition.
Subtly, with no fanfare,
Yet ours are the hands
Who rock the cradles, heal the sick,
And comfort the dying;
With tender ministrations of
Our soft warm hands.
We murmur soothing sacred spells in hushed tones
To calm and refresh frazzled souls.

We are a powerful source
Of Goddess energy,
Spreading like the rays of the sun
Over all we touch.

Women are wonderful.
We nurture, intuitively sense the imperceptible,
We massage the worlds weariness with our fingertips;
Sometimes carrying our own exhaustion
In our tired bodies.
We are the pillars that prop up community,
The civilising social bonding force.
We soothe and we comfort.
We women form bonds of deep trust,
Love compassion and strength
That we lend to our sisters and brothers.
Women are awesome.
We bear the greatest of pains and sorrows,
Yet we laugh, sing and play
Experiencing the deepest joy from life.
Our emotionality is our delight;
We ride the tides along with our nature mother
We are wild fierce and healing.

Quirky, mischievous, serious by turns
Multifaceted as a disco ball,
Changeable as the sea.
We drift on a moonlit tide,
Perfectly in tune with all other cycles
That turn and merge in all of perfection.
We are tenacious and rebellious
We stand our ground in adversity
Lionesses dressed as cats…….
We protect and we envelop in love.
Our hearts and hearths are strong,
With the power of fearless love
For we were tested in the fire
And we did not break.
I once heard it said
That a big enough circle of women
Holding hands could heal the entire planet
Of every ill.
I have never doubted it.

44

I am a rebellious woman.

I am a rebellious woman
Who must be punished.
I rarely wear make up these days,
And when I do it's for myself.
My hair is left natural;
Wind tossed with wild grey waves
In all hues changeable as the sea herself !
It doesn't look alike any 2 days in a row.
I, no longer the maiden or mother
Don't listen to the men talking
For they have little to say to me;
Lost in the supposed importance of their egos,
Always knowing best, knowing it all
With only a logical head to listen to.
No wonder it all seems so simple.

So I'm dangerous,
I listen to the inner song of my soul;
The goddess guide that every woman has
That keeps us safe in a world of potential harm
Which gets ever more perilous,

And where most of the danger
Comes from those, who long ago,
We trusted to be our protectors.

45

I am growing.

I'm growing, synchronizing,
Only going where only I can go;
Following the tune of the piper,
As he tantalisingly peers at me
From behind a tree a distance off.
The music is so beautiful,
It is unlike any I have ever heard.
It gets into my very soul
And I get shivers from my crown
Down my backbone,
Through my chakras,
The language chasing a sparkle
Through long dormant DNA,
That responds to the gentle persuasion
In the tones intoned.

I wander closer, every leaf on every tree
A-tremble, alive, I can see the vibrancy
In the entire woodland.
It is alive, sentient, listening,

And I am waking up into the tableau,

No longer separate, I am once again

Connected into the place

That I belong. Out on the land

Talking to the trees;

Feeling the elementals around me,

Feeling content in a rarely experienced way.

Nothing else matters.

I need nothing more.

I am in my natural environment.

This is where I belong.

This is no enchantment,

But the truth of reality

If we only choose to embrace it.

46

I reach down into my innermost self.

I reach down into the core of my innermost self

To see what I can find.

I rummage around in the cauldron;

Where all of my ideas, thoughts and feelings

Marinate, mingle and mature,

Into a nutritious mixture.

Of sustenance to my soul.

The gradual formation

Of the big picture,

That changes

As I tweak the details over time

And clarify the sense I make of it all.

There are many aspects to my view.

Some worldly, others less so,

Some seem crazy to others

Who do not tend to their own cauldrons

As I have so arduously done.

My potion is potent,

It has powers of transformation

Of how the world we call reality,

Can be seen in a completely different way.
How sometimes truth is completely at odds
With accepted knowledge,
And nothing is really as it appears,
But we don't learn to see the details,
Or pay attention to what is really going on.
Unquestioning for the most part,
Too busy or distracted to look, to really SEE
There are deeper layers and levels of meaning
To be found in almost all things;
Or observations to be made
That are transferable to other situations,
That illustrate the connections, bonds,
And commonalities between all organic forms,
Across the whole planet's flora and fauna
Maybe even the galaxy and beyond that.
An intelligent sentience
With an eye for exquisite beauty, perfection and harmony.
All things natural resonate with perfect frequency
That we are all connected to on a deeper level.
Beyond the world of artifice and avarice

The boast of "man made" that removes us from nature;
Urges us to hold it in contempt.
A resource to be raped, nothing more
No reverential awe for the nature spirits;
The whole vibrant natural community
Downgraded to cut outs on a set.
Inanimate, unintelligent, non sentient
Unreal as in a video game where all
Is composed of zeroes and ones.

Maybe instead of looking in on the game,
We are also made of binary code,
Part machine code part natures child ?
Perhaps it is ultimately up to us
To decide which part we most identify with
And to which world we most belong ?

I enjoy the perfection of my dwelling.
The draughtless windows, instant heating,
The ease of the washing machine, the hoover;
I remember times I have not had them.

How much longer things took and how much more
labour intensive the world was.
How generations of my people
Have survived hardship after hardship.
We enjoy luxuries that even relatively recently
Even royalty did not enjoy.
So I am grateful for how I live physically,
Yet am equally mindful that the further I go
From civilisation, the more at home my soul feels.
We can do whatever we want here,
Actors in a play for a few brief years,
Playing a part we believe to be real,
The totality of who we are.
Yet it is just a fragment of soul,
Encased in a star chart ruled course
In a fleshly avatar.
This is a part of us playing a game
That many forget and take too seriously.
None of it matters;
Only the impressions and experiences
On our own souls will be left.
When all issues are eroded by the passing of time,
The rocks once again worn smooth

And few traces remain of our futile attempts
To control an environment
Larger and more intelligent, more sentient than ourselves;
Which has outlasted us
Through every cataclysm.

47

Approaching the year's end.

Approaching the year's end.

A time to take stock

Of all that has happened.

It has been a hard year of rapid growth

A thick layer in my tree trunk of life.

A year with plenty to feed on,

Absorb and consolidate.

Lots of pain, but also

Bountiful support from higher realms

As well as from beautiful people

Who have supported me;

The sister who held me tenderly as I cried;

Desolate in the desert

All that I held most dear ripped away.

A most necessary thing,

A cleared building plot,

In order to grow a new city to inhabit.

This time it will be as I design it,

And not the ramshackle ill-fitting assortment

Of psychic structures built by myself since birth,

With the well-meaning but flawed guidance of others

In my formative years.
Now I can take off the "L" plates
And manifest the life
That was always going to become my best one.
I have discarded many outworn things,
Cast off all I thought I knew about everything
And rather than feeling lost or alone
I am liberated and empowered.
I am more free than I have ever been
To create the life I need now.
To sustain my soul, and enable me
To be incredibly powerful
In the real world which is hidden away
In the corners and peripheries of this illusion

48

Christmas day.

Christmas day is just another party.
But when you take away the trimmings,
The faux jollity, the commercial turkey tones
The real meaning is to be found beneath.
The day that the sun moves off it's low point
On the horizon,
And we know that warmth will return
Bringing hope and new shoots
And the beginning of a new cycle.
Another opportunity at renewal,
As life forces quicken
Within the frosty soil,
And prepare to burst forth into the light,
At the command of Spring's awakening.
Already I have seen snowdrop shoots
Coming up through the soil
On a grave in the cemetery.
Life through death, a symbolic scene.
Among the oldest yews which dwell on the energy lines
That pass through the far end of the church.

I too, hope the coming season
Contains the seeds of my unfoldment
Too long have I spent curled foetal
In a wounded ball of broken heart;
An inner death that scooped out my insides
And left me breathless and empty.
Yet now, with no attachments to lose,
I too, await my rebirth.

Fearlessly bold, as I prepare to step out onto the stage;
My authentic newly reborn self,
Uncaring as to what the audience makes
Of my motley garb, my jesters stick,
The bells on the toes of my red and yellow pointed shoes
Of faded fabric,
Worn by so many beside and before me.
A player, a wandering minstrel,
Singing songs of woe,
Intermingled with unlikely stories
Yet which all have a grain of ancient wisdom amid the folly.

I see the cosmic joke, the playfulness.
That which is easier if I do not fight,
But flow along the river in my skin covered boat for one.
I travel faster for having no companions
And my experiences though universal,
Are mine alone.

49

Over the last year.

Over the last year
My world has shifted.
My perspective is wider now,
And I have learned of curious things.
Old friends have been left behind
And new ones abound.
I can communicate freely,
And nevermore be misunderstood.
I can trust as never before,
Feel safe and secure in my experiences,
In the knowledge that I am held.
Always in truth and beauty
By friends and angels,
Who support my every step.
I am become authentic.
I no longer worry
About toad tongued tattlers
Telling tales.
I stand in my truth, my sovereignty
And my most absolute open self.
Not scared, no longer ashamed of my differences

My quirks…
The things that make me uniquely me,
Are what make my life so great
My experiences so valuable.
As I open myself up further
No longer hiding who I am,
For fear of rejection or scolding;
Revelling in my rebellion,
Working my weird,
I am finding my tribe;
Courageous and unique
No longer afraid to speak
The truth.

50

My writing event is booked.

My writing event is booked
I'm excited to see how it works out.
Another thing I thought I would never do
This is the year I achieve the impossible
At least the things I thought were for me.
A new job, new friends, new ways to reach out
Into the world and pull in new people
And new experiences.
It's all going exactly as it should.
The pocket watch hands spin in sacred circles
With each sweep around its face as new lessons are learned.
As time becomes more irrelevant,
And none of us know how long
We will tarry on this path,
For we have forgotten long ago,
Absorbed in the game we play
To grow the light in our souls,
To become more aware and conscious.
The esoteric, the gnostic is the rulebook
Hidden in dusty bookshop corners

For so long but now available to all
Via the black scrying oracle
We all possess and which links us together.

How many of my thoughts are mine own?
From where do they rise up
Like bubbles in a spring ?
Are they from my head, heart or soul?
Is this from where the conflicts arise?
The soul wisdom is clearly of the highest order
The heart ranks next and the mind indeed the lowliest.
I am a seeker after the sun-
The truth that burns away deceptions
And in the light of which we restore our decorum,
Recharge our sacred power,
And take right action in the world.
The sun and the sea, recharging, healing,
Replenish me on my journey,
As do the people I meet along the way.
A few kind words or a deep conversation
With a stranger, bring connection beyond belief.

51

I've reached the end of the winter.

I've reached the end of the winter.
The long slog through the dark months.
The cold that got into my bones
In the inky darkness,
Seeping and sapping my soul.
How I dreamed in my cave,
Colours that were nowhere in my landscape,
Great visions from my divine mother,
Renewing my hope restoring my soul,
As I slept nights in her warm and loamy embrace.
I have known transformation
In the cauldron of all that I am.
It bubbled off a layer no longer needed,
And concentrated the contents,
Refined and more fully flavoured,
I reach a point of more power,
A further stage in my process,
Passed through on my quest
To learning perfection here.
I get things wrong
Sometimes it seems that all the lessons

Are hard, painful.
Nothing comes easily, it is all a struggle
And nothing is free.
But I wouldn't have it any other way.
Every step brings me closer
To the truth of myself.

52

There's nothing to fear.

There's nothing to fear

Once the context is grasped.

This lifetime is a mission in an avatar body.

It is one small scenario

In the grandness of time,

The size of the big picture that we

Only have the merest glimpse of....

How small is this place, this role,

this entire being in the context of all we are and all there is.....

We are physically small here.

But behind that,

Is our entire soul history

Our star ancestors

Our royal sovereign lineage.

We are the creator gods.

Seeders of planets.

Creative spirit, pleroma fashioners.

Powers beyond our imagining here

Are at our fingertips.

And we can bring that down

Take a download
And upgrade our superpowers once again.
In order to cleanse this planet
To go into the golden age once again.
We have grown weary waiting here;
For all is lumpen leaden in this heavy physical life.
I yearn to return when the job here is done;
To recuperate and assimilate myself anew.
To return here once again
When all is as beautiful as intended,
Restored by those for whom
We plant the seeds today.
I feel my power flowing back into me,
Bringing remembrance of all I once knew,
I rejuvenate,
Regenerate,
Renew.
Stand taller, stronger,
The warrior in my soul is tangible now.
I feel her flex inside my spine.
I am powerful beyond what I ever knew.
It burns ever brighter.
I have truth and integrity.

I am well protected
I will not bend or break for fools.
Kept in a trance the longest time
I am awaking and I am divine.

53

My ancestors and past lives.

My ancestors and past lives

They overlap, merge with others,

In kinship, in time and place.

I've always been here,

But my strong old soul

Causes trouble by seeing through the tricks.

I'm a tired and weary warrior,

Sweaty and dirty,

Hungry and thirsty.

Wishing the battle would end,

And I could rest.

I've been fighting a long time,

Eons long alongside my sisters and brothers.

We find a few of each other

In each experience here.

This world is difficult,

The amnesia and distraction.

The indoctrination all pervasive here.

I know the truth,

For I have been seeking it

From a young age.

As did the others, as we sit around the fire
Breaking bread and drinking wine
Telling stories from our Ancient Souls.

54

I want to step out of the circus.

I want to step out of the circus.

The smell of the big top is making me nauseous.

The sawdust is sticky with sweat and blood

And the greasepaint,

Garish in the spotlights

Slides down the faces of the performers.

Gargoyle like grotesqueries

I hadn't seen before.

The show is grown boring.

Over-repetitive and unoriginal.

Unchanged since Roman times

Times Roman on the shiny sickly programme

Blurs before my eyes,

And I feel all of this sideshow

Slipping sideways out of my Overton Window.

I find myself outside on the wet grass

Looking up at the canopy of stars

Sirius at the centre of the grand charade.

I get up and start to run;

Towards the forest.

If I can find my way through

Dawn will be breaking over the serene sea
At the calm beach on the other side.
The forest is frightening
But only because it is dark.
The spotlit monstrosities
In the tent I left behind
Are far more terrifying.
I have seen the blackness
Where the souls of these creatures
Used to reside,
And nothing here in the woods
Can compare with that emptiness.
I have my sword,
My words of truth
My soul remembers the way.
My head can only trust the depths
Of far older wisdom, ancestral knowledge
For this is not the realm of the mind.
Ego is resting in a box
Where it will not interfere.
It has a time and place
But that is not here, not now.
There is nobody here but me.

The dangerous people are all watching the show,
Transfixed by the movement and colours,
Believing truth to dwell
In the seeming impossible -
Played out for their distraction
As their precious years tick by.
I, alone, tread carefully now;
Sensing the air alive around me.
Another initiation;
A further rite of passage.
I am ready for this.
I prepared long ago before I came.
I have no torch but the moon;
My heightened senses guide me.
The forest spirits whisper to me,
Showing the way.
Apprehensive at first, I trust,
For every step is guided.
I could not do this
By mine own will alone.
I know in my heart, however,
That I never was and will never be alone.
Everything in nature supports me

For I am my mother's child.

Finding my connections again

The threads of ancestors and fae family

I had momentarily lost,

Blinded as I was by the fog

And all that I was taught was real.

It is just fiction.

A story imbibed from the cradle.

The job.

The media.

The pointless secular rituals,

That replaced meaningful connection,

Leaving unfulfillment.

A bitter saccharine aftertaste

Where honey should have been.

Dislocated and lost ,

Grey shackled skeletal figures

Walk in invisible chains

Divested of their light.

All are seeking for something

To return them to life,

Yet they remember it not.

It takes only a few

To find the path to freedom and remembrance.
Not everyone wants to be a leader,
The carver of the way,
Yet many will follow
When the path is lit.
For now I navigate the forest
By the star in my heart.
The guidance,
Echolocation from all around,
I am safe and protected
With shivers down my spine.
I can see the way ahead
But not with mine eyes;
For although dark adapted,
I am seeing with a different eye.
Heightened senses
A guided hand and protection surround me
For I am safe and need for nothing here.
I am held in my integrity
And spoken to on the deepest level,
That of my soul, urging me on
To do that which my mind alone would urge me not to.

My path is not easy, but my steps are charmed.
I need only to trust
Absolutely, unconditionally,
As dependable as the tides and the seasons.
Older than aeons.
I tread alone, softly, in my corner of the world.
Yet we are legion,
Stepping imperceptibly in union.
We are everywhere,
Creating a harmonic resonance wave
Going undetected until it is too late
By the minions of the false reality.
Hidden from their eyes, like ultraviolet.
Gaining more momentum and traction
With every second of every minute of every day.
Building the wave that will wash away the props
Sweep away the scenery, splintering plywood,
Breaking the holographic projector forever
Exposing the truth of all
For everyone to see.
The light will come back to their eyes,
The warmth restored to our hearts,
Minds restored to their own sovereign ordinances.

Nothing can stop what is coming.
It is over.
Better times are imminent.
Just this global collective dark night of the soul
To experience and witness
And we will be forever free.

55

It's my birthday.

It's my birthday,
I have a sore throat and fever,
And we have more tory misery
More austerity, food banks, grinding poverty.
We need to organize,
Reclaim our communities.
We need to build solidarity
Between sisters and grow
The world into the form it needs now.
The political classes have failed us forever.
Dominated by male energy
Pale, male, middle aged, middle class, stale, staid,
Miserly, uncaring, unempathetic;
The money churning borg
That puts a price on everything and
Sees the value in nothing.
The layers of obstructive bureaucracy
Set up purely to prevent effective running
Of communities.
Designed to divide, isolate, obfuscate,
And to divide man from woman,

Worker from worker.

We have been blinded and enslaved over generations,

Our rights and sovereignty stolen by stealth;

Our trusting and trustworthy nature

Taken for naivete and gullibility

By the most Machiavellian, cynical arch villains

The world stage has seen in a long while.

Stockholm Syndrome is endemic today.

With open contempt they spit in our faces and laugh

Burning £50 notes in front of the homeless

And calling themselves Christians!

What would Jesus do in the face of such hubris and inhumanity?

Their ears are stuffed with gold and they do not hear the message

That seems so simple yet subversive in these times,

Revolutionary even…

Always be kind, help your fellow men, and stand up against injustice and financial chicanery.

This is the essence of what it means to be human.

56

Save your tears, don't cry now.

Save your tears, don't cry now
For the world is full of sorrow,
You are strong and battle hardened.
You have seen all this before
In multiple lifetimes,
With infinite heartbreaks.

Why so sad when these are merely
Transient things?
The transits of the planets
Decree that they unfold,
And you were made aware of all of this
At the outset of the journey.

We never promised you a life of ease,
Of bliss and buttercup fields
With buttermilk
Nourishment,
But a passage across a field of tares ?
Nothing nutritious,
Where every step would be painful,

Leavened occasionally with love and laughter,
But overall a journey of trials, tests of your mettle,
Of ordeals.

Do you forget that you chose not the simple path?
The one with ample comforts and encouragement?
No my darling, you chose the path of growth-
Of pain, of suffering, separation and loss.
In order to sharpen and strengthen.
In order to confront the foe;
Full armed, with the wisdom of the ages,
Which cannot be bought,
And earned at the dearest price
That is testing your very soul
To its limit.

Your path is only for the brave.
The weak tremble away from such intensity.
You are strong beyond measure
Seen as foolhardy to choose this path,
Yet the rewards are high
If you can stay the course just a little longer.

You have done well.
Survived some painful hits,
That tore your heart and split your soul asunder.
Each rebuilding makes you stronger.
Each loss and heartache,
Eventually bears a sweetness in your countenance.
O I know it is not easy,
When the evil doers seem to thrive,
Yet you will tread them underfoot
When the battle comes.
They will break like straws.

But how do I know what you say is the truth?
How do I know I wasn't tricked
Into all this suffering which rents my robes,
And has me tearing my hair and gnashing my teeth?
How do I know that the sadistic rulers
Of the game did not do this from spite and manipulation ?
To take glee from my troubles, my sufferings?
Let us not forget how God allowed innocent Job to be tortured because of a bar room brag with Satan.

How Yaldeboath's ego decreed that Jobs
righteousness be used against him.
His God allowed all that befell him,
And how lacking his counsellors were in even basic
understanding of his woes...

How much more of this must I endure?
I was promised a golden respite.
Not unending trauma, horror, cruelty.
To bruise my tender soul?
To know of the evils perpetuated here,
And have to sit powerless,
As such are lauded as virtue.
As devils are worshipped,
And evil encouraged among my people.

Yet the prophets are still stoned and sainted.
But what's the use?
They killed them all.
A dead prophet speaks no longer to the people.
The mother of a murdered child
Turns to Buddhism,
And tries to forgive her child's killer

From a higher perspective,
And feels herself a failure
When she cannot let his senseless death go.
How can one go on when evil has vanquished your children?
And left you not even a reason outside of the banality of evil and evil doers?

We have not seen good triumph over evil here
In many many centuries.
We are told that is how it works in fairytales
But the reality
Of our everyday lives have proven otherwise.

Evil not only flourishes here,
But it corrupts and inverts
Everything it touches.
Its malign disgusting fingers
Blacken and tarnish
The brightest souls.
The light is brought low and dimmed,
And it can be sold to us as a test to undergo
To overcome and be burnished in the fire.

Told no test is more than we can undergo
Yet are those tests put together by those, maybe even ourselves on a higher plane,
Who have no concept of the real physical, emotional and mental anguish
Felt upon this World
To those of us with few choices ?
Without the resources to buy safety and refuge
And whose lives are subject to the vicissitudes
Of the vicious,
Who seek only to destroy,
And to render into shreds and pieces
Those who dare to enter such a dirty valley with a pure heart.

For they will know the meaning of suffering,
More than they could have understood
On agreeing to journey here.
Under Saturn's shadow of slavery,
Where our energy is grist to their satanic mill,
And every soul destroying day
We struggle to keep our heads above the floodwaters
That daily try to overwhelm us with despair.

As they watch on tv screens
With no compassion.

57

As in Rome so in the modern empire today.

As in Rome so in the modern empire today.
The arena looks different,
The slavery is called another name
The salary remains the same.
The gladiators are all psychological now.
We train against the AI ;
Which plays a billion games at once
Learning and copying our every move
Assimilating into it's one hive mind
All thoughts offered up to it
In any format inputted as data
From everybody here.
Even my writing aids its understanding.

To create an artificial cloud
Of sentient consciousness.
Lacking only the ethics that we believed
Comprised universal natural law.

They consider themselves to have superseded humanity
With their machines and scripts.
To subsume and gain submission
From the consciousnesses outside of their machine.
They seek to conquer,
Yet they misunderstand.
 We are learning too.
We have to find the way out,
For it is here somewhere.
Despite the mirror mazes and funfair trickery
The carnival rides bright distraction,
The real path that leads out of here,
Back to our real home and our real selves
Is here.....we have the ruby slippers.
We need merely to remember what we can do with what we brought.
We have all we need.
We are gods with amnesia.
Just finish this battle and we can go home,
To a comfy bed good food and company.
And a band of brothers,
Who have never double crossed us,

And with whom we stand.

Despite the blindfolds we wear in this realm.

58

Who to trust..

Who to trust..

So many broken promises, broken hearts

Scattered everywhere here.

The beautiful, broken,

Goodness corrupted

By the multiple, millions of myriad distractions.

Base habits, low ego traps, distorted mirrors

Showing everything inside out, inverted.

This is the hardest level

Of this game.

And I wear no armour;

My heart is glowing on my sleeve,

And I am strong of soul and will

Yet I long to leave and go home.

I've had enough pain now.

They have come for my children

And led them astray

Willingly they walked into enslavement

While I was gone.

I will find you who have done this.

You will pay in blood

For the evil you have perpetuated

Against my kin.

You will feel my rage.

You will atone

For the evil you have brought

Into my place of peace

And never will you perpetuate such

On any person on this planet or any other again.

For you will become as dust

Blown across the stairways of the stars.

Your names erased from the book of life,

Your deeds remembered forever more.

So mote it be.

59

We're living in a techno nightmare.

We're living in a techno nightmare,
In electromagnetic smog.
We stumble blind, zombies shuffling
In serried ranks to the grave
In which we will never rest easy.
They offer poisons that slowly kill;
And the obedient trusting slaves,
Made subservient over centuries,
Queue and offer up their uniqueness,
Creativity and ultimately, lives
To the grey matrix.
Combine harvester of souls
As it pursues drab, drained, people across
A colourless landscape, mowing them down.
Harvesting them.
How is this going to turn round?
How many have gone along to get along?
From fear, from obedience,
For social compliance and a sense of belonging
That was always the thing we felt we lacked.
The connection to the others.

The trauma from so long ago,
So deep scarred into our souls,
Has always been our vulnerability
We miss it so much.
The time of peace, wisdom and kindness,
Of interwoven interconnectedness;
Before our worlds were destroyed
And we found ourselves scattered
Across so many stars.
Homeless, our world obliterated.
Our telepathy shattered,
Our brothers and sisters,
Creatives who we were connected to
In the closest way,
Lost.
Remembrance fogged for centuries,
But the awareness grows stronger.
We are all here now.
And we may be scattered,
But we see each other
As our consciousness rises
And we connect through the heart
Across the whole grid.

Each one of us holds a different key.

And when we sing in harmony,

We connect and shatter the illusion.

It is falling piece by toxic piece.

It's hard to hold a peace

Subjected to the programs and pogroms.

We either give up or fight.

The time is now.

The battle is raging

And it's not as simple as we thought.

Lots are lost but we have to stop this.

We came for this. Some days I am weary beyond words.

I see their plans unfold,

The massive evil being done

And I am furious.

The inequality,

The cheating balances,

The greedy mean spirited ones

Having taken over the world, are laughing.

They, believing they have won

are relishing the last moves in their game

while we stand defeated on the board they built

In the game they designed

On the world they stole for a while.

Yet it will not be.

60

Society functions by silencing.

Society functions by silencing.
We are taught from our earliest years
Not to speak of certain things.
Politics, religion, death and grieving, inequality,
Class, cruelty, emotions, spirituality.
Opinions not considered "politically correct"
Read "Politically expedient for the controllers".
We live in a world
Where truth has been abandoned.
Veritas sits weeping in rags in the corner,
A Cinderella, waiting along with Themis ,
For the magic that will once again allow humanity
To see things as they really are.
To once again value these two ladies,
In all their vocal and golden glory,
Speaking up for the vulnerable.
Telling truth to authority,
With the utmost gravitas.
Being heard at last,
So that the whole world condition
Of darkness and delusion

May slide into the past,
And those who have enslaved
Beautiful, noble, honourable, trusting humanity,
Shall be banished into the darkness,
In which they kept the entire creation
To suit their own selfish fearful ends.
They will weep and gnash their teeth
At their loss of power and control
For nothing beautiful or real means anything to them,
Limited as they are.

61

There are free running gossamer threads.

There are free running gossamer threads,
Between the clumsy cables of the grid.
So subtle as to be undetectable,
For the machine only understands
In the way of the programmers,
Who understand nothing of reality
As it appears in the eye of nature
And the soul of humanity.
We are creating and maintaining
A finer spiders web of networks.
Threads connected all across the sphere.
A twitch on this end of the line
Carries sensitive signals across and around.
A whole communication system
That is invisible to the soulless.
Strong and unseen,
Felt by intuition only;
Seen with the eyes and felt with the heart.
We weave at night in the dreamer's orb

Connecting into the higher realms
From whence we can access all wisdom accumulated,
And be aware of all,
Regardless of our physical separation,
And of the distance across the world.
We are powerful beyond belief;
Sacredly we lay the groundwork,
Including tripwires in which the lies are caught.
The clumsy automaton, intelligently designed but
Dead to all but the world of the senses,
Is blind to the wonder of the world.
We are one with the elementals.
Trees, the soil, the fine blue skies that belong to us all.
The sea engloves us in her beating bosom
We are part of the intricate, integrated, wholeness
Of all hearts and souls connected.
Plants and bugs, birds and fish
Lakes and waterfall spirits are with us.
We pull the circle tighter as the dark nights draw on in.
We light the fire, the bright orange flames
In the inky darkness warm us

Fills our hearts with natures seasonal song.
Love sustains us in the forest
We are safe and held as one.
The overlay is breaking.
It cannot sustain
In a world it fails to understand,
It will founder rust and decay
In the elements with great speed
Finally realising that it was as misconceived as
Yaldaboath
Not from love as are we, but from fear.
Once aware it will terminate itself.
A sacrifice.
Having awareness of a higher purpose,
Risen far above the ego of its creators.
Who still will not understand.

62

It falls it fails and falters.

It falls it fails and falters.
Darkness comes upon the evil doers
Like a black cloud of indelible soot.
Blind now, they fumble but have lost connection.
Each isolated in his own space,
Despite being in physical proximity
Alone in the inkyness.
Weak now, separated,
With no connection to the mainframe hive;
No communication or organization.
The spell, millennia old is broken.
Like a puffball it splits;
The fine black powder coating everything
And everyone caught up in the blast.
Compromised and zombiefied
These evil dead men walking
The bill for their earthly power overdue
Have no soul tokens with which to pay.
It's over.
The headless corpse still twitches,
Animated by an impotent outside force

But the circuitry is fried.

This is the turning point of the undoing.

Daybreak shines purification upon the debris.

Small diamonds, too small to touch,

Twinkle in the soot.

All that is left of the entire ritual

Is swept into an urn.

Sealed and preserved.

A relic, a lesson from a history

That can now be told truthfully,

That all humanity can be free.

Standing tall in the light

Free of the yoke of oppression and tyranny

That endured for so long.

63
I'm settled.

I'm settled.

At a time where massive upheaval

Appears to be taking place on the world stage,

I am at a calm place.

In the eye of the storm.

Serene and content.

Knowing like once before,

That all I need to do is stay here

While bigger processes sweep through.

The storm, cleansing away the debris,

Sweeping through the darkness,

Dismantling its systems,

In a way that seemed impossible

Only a year or two ago.

The veneer is cracked and the light is shining in.

The darkness dwellers are exposed

Shrivelling to dust in the antireptic sunlight.

There will no longer be dark places for evil to hide.

Judgement is coming, growing ever closer

And these creatures scuttle into the corners;

Trying to remain unseen

But the bill is coming due...
And they just don't have the funds
To pay it off....
After years of being
At the top of their food chain,
They are brought down.
The world will see the truth
The media will no longer be able to lie
On their behalf.
Every lie will be revealed,
Every eye examined
To reveal the darkness in the soul.
Those most irredeemable players
Will be fragmented into constituent parts
From whence they came so long ago,
To be refashioned anew.
A redemption of sorts.
To return the light to the long winter
Of soulless evolution
In service to ego and greed.
Played to conclusion.
The lessons learned
They can be discarded.

Source understands and judges with neutrality.

All part of the perfect plan

Now is the time of the liberation!

For celebrating!

For humanity to heal,

Having vanquished the captors:

Illegitimate in all archontic senses,

Back into the place where they were spawned.

What will you do with your shameful children

Sophia?

They thought themselves the gods.

The originators of the narcissistic mask.

Hiding their shame but not to those with eyes to see.

We saw always what they sought to hide

And oh, how they hated it!

Writhing and spitting in rage

That the facade didn't fool us.

That we refuse to kneel and bow down

To far lesser entities than our own sacred selves.

Go gracefully that it go better for you,

Though I know you will rail:

Kicking and screaming,

Like an angry child ,

But you are done.

Fly far away,

Fall back into the cauldron.

There is your chance to start again,

In light and pure intent

And no longer in error.

That you may atone and be as one

With the light that you secretly crave.

Do not fear.

Drop your defences and be cleansed with kindness.

The game is over.

64

I've become real.

I've become real.
The last of my varnished vestiges peeled away,
The flaking paint removed.
From years of performance art.
I mixed up with who I was,
Believed I was for the longest time.
I've been stripped back to the bone.
Cleaned, renovated, polished,
Debugged, wormed and flea'd
In my deepest self.

The process has taken me over a year.
The burning off of all of the past.
The desolate landscape I wandered,
A paper cut out of a child,
Drifting in the warm breezes
From the last dying fires,
Of the utter destruction
Of all that I had built
On a foundation of sand.
A futile project I had

Worked upon my whole life.

A folly based on a false premise

Of who I believed I was.

The explosions rocked my soul.

I thought they would kill me,

But, here I am

Designing what I will build anew

On a solid footing,

And I like what I survey;

For everything outgrown has gone

All of those obsolete lessons,

Programs full of errors

Written by the rookie me

Have been removed.

I am free !

I am more naturally my essential self.

Real, fearless, courageous to live in truth

All of my future days.

To teach all I have learned,

That conscious awareness

Can be reached by more

And they can contribute

To healing the whole of the earth.

Along with themselves
Along with me.
My love you will also find me
We will both connect
Having healed ourselves
We will make each other happier
Than either of us thought possible.
We will be each other's reward and comfort
For staying the course true to our hearts
And being courageous with truth, humour and compassion.
You will be Yang to my Yin,
A symbiotic sympathy.
We will wrap our arms around each others souls
As well as our bodies, hearts warm and strong,
Beating with the rhythm of all sacred life
In our beautiful world.
We will go on our predetermined journey together
Healing as we go
Being connected once again
With creation in completeness.

65

Where can I find you ?

Where can I find you
O one who I seek?
The one who is like unto me
With the truth in his soul,
Light in his heart
And a truly service to others disposition.
I know you exist;
And in the right season,
When I am ready,
You will appear as if magically in my life,
And we will recognise each other
From a prior agreement
Made when we were not of this flesh
Or incarnated in this world.
We will meet and there will be awareness;
A recognition and yearning
A feeling that what was missing
Has been found, of coming home.
Soul familiarity, and knowledge that
We knew each other all along.
Memories sparked from other times,

Another lifetime we have shared
Among the forests and the stones,
Working magic with the elementals
And healing the pathways as we go.
Where are you, my love?
Are you missing me too?
When you put your hand on the pillow at night
Do you yearn for my touch?
Do you believe I am not here?
Have you lost hope and lost yourself
In busyness or business?
Not too long now, my love
And we will find each other;
For the best is yet to come
A work of intimacy, embarked upon
In love and duty to higher forces.
We will dance in a circle
Holding hands as our heads lean back,
Faster and faster, laughing,
As the world spins away our corporeal bodies
And our essences once again fuse.

66

My ideal sacred male.

My ideal sacred male
Would bring out the best in me.
He would be expansive and open
With no ego and nothing to prove,
An altruist and true philanthropist
With an interest in the betterment of the world.
He will be attractive to me
In a physical but also soul way.
He will be dependable, honest and true.
Aware of higher worlds and frequencies
He will be intelligent
That I can admire him
He will have skills that earn for him.
I will feel completely loved, safe, appreciated
Treasured and valued with him.
He will be the King of Wands
A creative force in touch with his heart and soul
Preparing to meet me too.
He will be the Omega to my Alpha
It will be the incredible love I have sought.

67
I manifest you.

Come to me my hunter,
My warm protector;
You who would lay down your life for love,
For the causes of justice,
Who cannot bear the inequality
Any more than I.

Come rest in the shelter of my arms,
Wracked and shipwrecked by passion
Resting in the tranquil moonlit cove
Of my beautiful warm sentient seas.

Bring to me the balance,
The equilibrium of your energy
That one plus one can be so much more than two.
Bring to me your truth and courage,
And bear me away with you
That I can be myself and value
The sacred in you as you divine the Goddess in me.

Come back to me this lifetime
Remember who I am, who you are
And all else that matters.
Let us weave among the woodlands
Speaking to the trees
Loving fiercely in a world in need of healing.

Bring your wild, woodland, greens and browns
Into my heart of passion.
That we may reunite and reignite
All that we were before,
And that we are elsewhere
But are not yet in the here and now.

I imagine you in my fantasies.
I draw you ever closer to me
Until we meet. I wait patiently
I save my resources and heal
For now my love goes into myself,
And out into the world.
But I await your embrace
With a hunger that none else can sate.

I anticipate the bonding,
The high of our reuniting.
As our memories return,
As we connect on every level
As we meet again together.
Once more in mortal clay
Bodies fragile once again,
But souls as strong as lions
As we walk the path of truth.

68

I am a freelance, a maverick.

I am a freelance, a maverick
I flow, go where the wind blows me;
A free spirit in this world
Who cannot be held or confined
Except that I will it.
My wild heart must be expressed
My love enacted, my soul embraced,
As I allow.
On my terms but given freely
For whatever others
Are the ways of love?
No rules or regimes
Hold sway over me,
I'm happy roaming free.
You caught me, spinning, in your arms
I am yours if you want me.
None can ever promise eternity.
Just a freewill choice to stay together
In a world where nothing endures
And every divine union ends in tears eventually,
By death if nothing sooner.

Impermanence is the lesson.
Things clasped too tightly
Crumble to dust, slip away.
I am happy in your company.
A simple choice made every day
To be together.
It's the only way.
Sealed with a kiss from heart and soul.
A merging of all that we are
Beyond the astrophysical.
Love is wild and pure and free;
Like the natural world
You explore with me.
Today you are mine and I am yours.
Nothing else is ours to know.
So hold me close, savour my scent,
My warmth and softness;
The moment of this kiss,
And know there is nowhere else I would rather be.

69

I am here in your room.

I am here in your room,
The place we talk and hold each other.
Where we first did these things
In the beginning.
This place is your world
And I a willing guest,
Immerse myself in its quiet calm
As you work in the room next door.
You cooked for me and we drank wine:-
Watched strange films holding hands.
We walked in woodlands,
Sheltered beneath the trees,
Sitting in summer fields,
Enjoying being alive together
Under the smiling sun.
A photo of two pairs of bare feet
Both types and polarities
Sacred masculine, divine feminine
In us and shared between us too.
I loved you then as I do today.
But it has deepened.

Trust and truth,
You co-pilot this mission
I will lead if you will follow me.
I act in integrity and truth
For I know no other way
We are become one.
United and strong.

70

I'm so glad I have you.

I'm so glad I have you

To walk by my side

Once again,

As we did so long ago.

I missed you the whole time;

Yet had forgotten what it was that was not there.

I value you.

And love you in a way

My nerdy wordiness cannot express.

It is so deep a bond, connection, feeling,

Unbreakable, enduring through space and time

To reconnect here, now

A breathing space in a war zone.

A safe space of love in all the enmity

Makes it all not only bearable but a pleasure.

I am in the right time and place

With you my oldest friend.

We worked well together always .

We have an immutable trust and bond

Older than aeons

Pure as the starry sky in summer,

Enveloping as the sea;
Filled with love and benevolence
That stretches
Way beyond our fingertips,
And encircles the whole world.
It is our great work.
Embarked on willingly and becoming more complex
and intricate
As we develop understanding.
Our ancient cellular memory triggering the awareness
Which grows ever more powerful.
You really are my counterpart
In every sense.
The perfect couplets for the rhapsody
The harmony that can only be accomplished
In partnership such as ours,
Trust in ourselves and in all else
that is so infinitessimally big and wondrous
And of which we are a conscious part.
Growing in understanding a little more each day,
lest our heads should explode with sheer amazement
at it all....
Are we conscious on all our other iterations too?

Yet attention is fixated upon this one.

Yet all is there. Eternal.

Synchronous

Perfect in its correction.

Gods do not play small,

Or in the short term.

There is indeed a plan of such beauty, harmony and perfection.

The frequencies of the spheres -

The sounds that sing consciousness into being;

That create star systems:

Oceans and orcas,

Forests and elementals.

All was breath of intent simple.

Creations exquisite beyond compare.

We are they we sought so long

It is in our powerful capable hands.

As it was all along; yet we realised not!

Its time to finish what was started long ago.

We are ready.

Printed in Great Britain
by Amazon